For Geraldine, Joe, Naomi,
Eddie, Laura and Isaac
M.R.

For Amelia
H.O.

Published by arrangement with

Walker Books Ltd, London
Dual language edition first published 2000
by Mantra Lingua Ltd
Global House, 303 Ballards Lane, London N12 8NU
www.mantralingua.com

This edition 2015

Printed in Paola, Malta MP250815PB09157211

ہم ریچھ کی تلاش میں جارہے ہیں

We're Going on a Bear Hunt

Retold by

Michael Rosen

Illustrated by

Helen Oxenbury

MANTRA
LINGUA

ہم ریچھ کی تلاش میں جا رہے ہیں۔
ہم بڑا سا ریچھ پکڑیں گے۔
کتنا خوبصورت دن ہے!
ہمیں ڈر تو نہیں لگ رہا ہے۔

We're going on a bear hunt.
We're going to catch a big one.
What a beautiful day!
We're not scared.

آ۔ہا! گھاس!
لمبی لہراتی گھاس۔
ہم اِس کے اُوپر سے نہیں جا سکتے۔
ہم اِس کے نیچے سے نہیں جا سکتے۔

Uh-uh! Grass!
Long wavy grass.
We can't go over it.
We can't go under it.

اوہ نہیں!
ہمیں تو اِس کے درمیان سے جانا ہو گا!

Oh no!
We've got to go through it!

سوئی شی سواشی!

سوئی شی سواشی!

سوئی شی سواشی!

Swishy swashy!
Swishy swashy!
Swishy swashy!

ہم ریچھ کی تلاش میں جا رہے ہیں۔
ہم بڑا سا ریچھ پکڑیں گے۔
کتنا خوبصورت دن ہے!
ہمیں ڈر تو نہیں لگ رہا ہے۔

We're going on a bear hunt.
We're going to catch a big one.
What a beautiful day!
We're not scared.

آ۔ ہا! ایک دریا!

ایک گہرا ٹھنڈا دریا۔

ہم اِس کے اُوپر سے نہیں جاسکتے۔

ہم اِس کے نیچے سے نہیں جاسکتے۔

Uh-uh! A river!
A deep cold river.
We can't go over it.
We can't go under it.

اوہ نہیں!

ہمیں اِس کے درمیان سے جانا پڑے گا!

Oh no!
We've got to go through it!

سپلیش سپلوش!

سپلیش سپلوش!

سپلیش سپلوش!

Splash splosh!
Splash splosh!
Splash splosh!

ہم ایک ریچھ کی تلاش میں جا رہے ہیں۔
ہم ایک بڑا سا ریچھ پکڑیں گے۔
کتنا خوبصورت دن ہے!
ہمیں ڈر تو نہیں لگ رہا ہے۔

We're going on a bear hunt.
We're going to catch a big one.
What a beautiful day!
We're not scared.

آ۔ہا۔ کیچڑ!

گاڑھی اُبلتی ہوئی کیچڑ۔

ہم اِس کے اُوپر سے نہیں جا سکتے۔

ہم اِس کے نیچے سے نہیں جا سکتے۔

Uh-uh! Mud!
Thick oozy mud.
We can't go over it.
We can't go under it.

اوہ نہیں!

ہمیں اِس کے درمیان سے جانا ہوگا!

Oh no!
We've got to go through it!

سکویلچ سکورچ!
سکویلچ سکورچ!
سکویلچ سکورچ!

Squelch squerch!
Squelch squerch!
Squelch squerch!

ہم ایک ریچھ کی تلاش میں جارہے ہیں۔
ہم ایک بڑا سا ریچھ پکڑیں گے۔
کتنا خوبصورت دن ہے!
ہمیں ڈر تو نہیں لگ رہا ہے۔

We're going on a bear hunt.
We're going to catch a big one.
What a beautiful day!
We're not scared.

آ۔ہا!ایک جنگل!

ایک بڑاسااندھیراجنگل۔

ہم اِس کے اُوپر سے نہیں جاسکتے۔

ہم اِس کے نیچے سے نہیں جاسکتے۔

Uh-uh! A forest!
A big dark forest.
We can't go over it.
We can't go under it.

اوہ نہیں!

ہمیں اِس کے درمیان سے جانا پڑے گا!

Oh no!
We've got to go through it!

سٹمبل ٹرپ!
سٹمبل ٹرپ!
سٹمبل ٹرپ!

Stumble trip!
Stumble trip!
Stumble trip!

ہم ایک ریچھ کی تلاش میں جا رہے ہیں۔
ہم ایک بڑا سا ریچھ پکڑیں گے۔
کتنا خوبصورت دن ہے!
ہمیں ڈر تو نہیں لگ رہا ہے۔

We're going on a bear hunt.
We're going to catch a big one.
What a beautiful day!
We're not scared.

آ۔ ہا ! ایک برف کا طوفان !

ایک گھومتا ہوا چکر کاٹتا ہوا برف کا طوفان ۔

ہم اس کے اُوپر سے نہیں جا سکتے ۔

ہم اس کے نیچے سے نہیں جا سکتے ۔

Uh-uh! A snowstorm!
A swirling whirling snowstorm.
We can't go over it.
We can't go under it.

اوہ نہیں !

ہمیں اِس کے درمیان سے جانا پڑے گا !

Oh no!
We've got to go through it!

ހޫ ވވވ ޫވވވ!

ހޫ ވވވ ޫވވވ!

ހޫ ވވވ ޫވވވ!

Hooo woooo!
Hoooo woooo!
Hoooo wooo!

ہم ایک ریچھ کی تلاش میں جا رہے ہیں۔

ہم ایک بڑا سا ریچھ پکڑیں گے۔

کتنا خوبصورت دن ہے!

ہمیں ڈر تو نہیں لگ رہا ہے۔

We're going on a bear hunt.
We're going to catch a big one.
What a beautiful day!
We're not scared.

آ۔ ہا ! ایک غار!

ایک تنگ تاریک غار۔

ہم اِس کے اُوپر سے نہیں جاسکتے۔

ہم اِس کے نیچے سے نہیں جاسکتے۔

Uh-uh! A cave!
A narrow gloomy cave.
We can't go over it.
We can't go under it.

اوہ نہیں!

ہمیں اِس کے درمیان سے جانا پڑے گا!

Oh no!
We've got to go through it!

ٹپ ٹو!

ٹپ ٹو! ٹپ ٹو!

وہ کیا ہے؟

Tiptoe!
Tiptoe! Tiptoe!
WHAT'S THAT?

ایک چمکتی ہوئی گیلی ناک!

دو بڑے بالوں سے بھرے کان!

دو بڑی بڑی گول گول آنکھیں!

یہ تو ایک ریچھ ہے!!!

One shiny wet nose!
Two big furry ears!
Two big goggly eyes!
IT'S A BEAR!!!!

جلدی کرو! واپس غار کے اندر چلیں! ٹپ ٹو! ٹپ ٹو! ٹپ ٹو!

Quick! Back through the cave! Tiptoe! Tiptoe! Tiptoe!

برف کے طوفان کے درمیان سے چلیں! ہُو ووو! ہُو ووو ہُو ووو ُووو! ہُو ووو ُووو!

Back through the snowstorm! Hoooo wooooo! Hoooo wooooo!

جنگل کے درمیان سے واپس چلیں! سٹمبل ٹرپ! سٹمبل ٹرپ! سٹمبل ٹرپ!

Back through the forest! Stumble trip! Stumble trip! Stumble trip!

کیچڑ کے درمیان سے واپس چلیں! سکوچلچ سکورچ ! سکوچلچ سکورچ !

Back through the mud! Squelch squerch! Squelch squerch!

دریا کے درمیان سے واپس چلیں! سپلیش سپلوش! سپلیش سپلوش!

Back through the river! Splash splosh! Splash splosh! Splash splosh!

گھاس کے درمیان سے واپس چلیں! سوئشی سوائشی! سوئشی سوائشی!

Back through the grass! Swishy swashy!

سامنے کے دروازے تک چلو۔

دروازہ کھولو۔ اُوپر سیڑھیوں پر چلو۔

اوہ نہیں! ہم دروازہ بند کرنا بھول گئے۔

نیچے چلو۔

Get to our front door.
Open the door. Up the stairs.

Oh no! We forgot to shut the front door.
Back downstairs.

دروازہ بند کرو۔ سیڑھیوں پر واپس چڑھو۔
سونے کے کمرے میں چلو۔

بستر کے اندر۔
لحاف کے نیچے۔

Shut the door. Back upstairs.
Into the bedroom.

Into bed.
Under the covers.

اب ہم کبھی ریچھ کی تلاش میں نہیں جائیں گے۔

We're not going on a bear hunt again.